THE SOUP BOWL
and other poems

Raja Chakraborty

Hawakal Publishers

Published by Hawakal Publishers, 185 Kali Temple Road, Nimta, Kolkata 700049

Email: info@hawakal.com

Website: www.hawakal.com

Copyright © Raja Chakraborty 2018
Cover image: *Canva*
Cover designed by Bitan Chakraborty

First edition (India): November, 2018

ISBN: 978-93-87883-39-0 (Paperback)

Price: INR 250
US Dollar 8.99

Neeloo
and
Kiriti Sengupta
who ceaselessly inspired me until I came up
with this collection

CONTENTS

A CANDLE BURNS

a candle burns
and gathers
dew drops
until the wicker
finds ground zero
no ashes for
the epitaph
no eulogy
in the air
just a flickering
halo timidly
tells the story
of a fire
that once jived
with the breeze
only to die
in a whisper

A PARADOX CALLED LOVE

the road narrowed
into a tight corner
where light and shadow
met
in a shaky embrace
behind the
moss-infiltrated wall
sharing space with
darkness and spider webs
hidden from trespassing
eyes
and fled
before the night fell
into eternity

.

ALONE

staccato bursts of
cryptic words
fell from her lips
in a gibberish heap
forming puddles of
unformed sentences
at her feet and mixed
with her tears
her eyes cried in
silence
alone

nobody listened until
the rivulets plunged
into the ocean and lost
identity
forever
and
a love went unheard

ASHES AND BONES

in the ground below
beneath your feet
behind the struggle of
grasses lies
truth untouched

and tells the
story of ashes
and bones that
once made us

BLACKOUT

do not light
the lamps
friend

in shadow
life is born

in darkness
it will end

THE BOHEMIAN

see how the wind plays
with fire
flirting with the flame

like a bohemian heart tempts the
feet to the gorge
and the drop below

like the tune that beckons and
you dance unmindful of your
blue-collar routine
midday
in trance

consumed in your own energy
you become the sun

fire burns itself in the end
ashes fly with the wind
you find your road
to a new end

no tears to cry
no bonds to break

BOUNDARIES

it is raining
dew drops are ashamed
they couldn't match the beads
or icicles poised

but then I thought
does sorrow have a limit
or is there a limit to which you cry

BURIED

when winds picked up
I used to hurry in shutting
the windows
precious china on the corner table
photo-frames carrying memories
fragile moments
is all that I cared for

lying under the unforgiving
concrete slab in an alien
darkness
numb
disoriented
I so wish for a little blob of
air for my bursting lungs
god I will never shut
your windows again
if you let me open this one

CLOWN

deep down
I'm a clown
and you know
that too

smile I spread is often fed
by tears I couldn't do

DEVIL AND I

I traded my soul
to the devil
for tidbits
now and then

a wish here
a desire there
some sops to
ease the pain

day by day
part by part
transformed
thus we stand

the devil prays
for salvation
and now I
wear his band

DO YOU HEAR

along the stone walls
footsteps echo and
whisper of souls that
once breathed within
these empty rooms
vacated by time

they tell stories of family
feuds and heroic battles
of romance and sacrifices

a desolate
pigeon flutters by
disturbed by the curious
shutter click
intruding

and in that moment of
erstwhile solitude
you are transported
back in time
when you used to be a hero
or perhaps could have been

you catch the flight back
to your city and routine

17

obscurity
the memory
remains and the image
of a lone warrior
fighting

DREAMS

I have kept some dreams
neatly tucked on an attic shelf
in an envelope

in my dreams I play with them
water them every monsoon and dry
them in the summer sun
the winter breeze ruffles them

some evenings I hear whispers
dreams call out
they want to see light
they struggle to open the lid
the glue holds on strong

I sit tight in the comfort of my corner
the envelope remains untouched
in ageless dust it has found home

I have never opened the envelope
for dreams can be nightmares in disguise

I sit still in the corner

ECLIPSE

bizarre clouds weave patterns
blown away by careless wind
remnants of a half-eaten sun disappeared

devilish moon
what will satiate your hunger for light

ECTOPLASM

tiny parts of me
slowly evaporated
through epidermis
traveled in ether
floating like dew
drops in the air

found your pores
to dissolve in you

soul to soul
blood to blood
we mated
on a new moon night
one shadow to light

FROZEN

frozen
in an
embryo
I have kept
a life
yet to be
touched
by the sun
or our sins

let it sleep
unpolluted

GHOST WALKERS

walking on the grass barefooted
she touched her soul
naked blades tickling her senses
arousing her to the colors of spring
and sounds of blooming flowers
she smiled to herself
alive in her thought

such are the images of an innocent life
cut short
abrupt in its cruelty
still vibrant in conversation of the living

where the line between this world
and the other is vague
obscene almost

INERTIA

in this life or the other
oceans in between
and a hell or a heaven
lie two selves for us to find
and we keep going
in never ending circles of birth
and rebirth

still fail to fathom the meaning
of our existence
and stuck like a
cobweb
hang midair
between two worlds
forever

KEEP GOING ON

the road ate
into unknown miles
relentless
straight
as an arrow
going nowhere

yet I trudged on
for life is a series of travelogues
written by nomadic souls
in sand

LET THE PYRE BURN

let the pyre burn
and engulf all
that was close to me
I have promised
not to cry

few unintended tears
let them speak
of joy and
the life we had
in sunshine

LOOKING BACK

marbles and spins made my day
a few decades back
the sky was my empire
my throne a random stack
we drenched naked in raindrops
like there's no tomorrow
we laughed for no reason
and cried in others' sorrow
we sang together in harmony
out of tune and words
we chased wild dreams and
flew with the birds
we ran barefooted
to catch the butterflies
we were no angels though
and had our share of lies
we were rivers of life
each horizon a new home
looking back still brings a smile
in this world of concrete and chrome
and sitting alone in darkness
my mind silently says
why you had to grow up
'coz those were the days

MASKS

cobwebs from the past
clustered his morning face
fluffy from a ragged
perturbed sleep

red eyes bore into the
dream he had

masks
he was dreaming of
absent minded
he put on one
he will be god today
next to none

MEMOIRS OF A MUDDLED MIND

hammer and chisel in hand
I etch out words from everyday moments
rinse them with memories and
paint them in dreams
I take them one by one
put them on your lap

hoping someday the fog will clear
and in your moments of clarity
you'll see the picture of a man
and a woman in embrace
and say wish they were us
until then I keep making words
for you

MEMORIES

do the returning waves take back
memories of the shore

does the moon remember its deaths
eclipse by eclipse or re-birth.

does the soul ever long for the shell
it left for another

do memories die or live on like the north star,
fading away to appear again

stones that hold in their breasts
footprints of time

MERRY-GO-ROUND

there goes the merry-go-round
drawing circles in the air

joy and sorrow arm in arm
cushioned in its chair

with each turn laughter spread
and turned into a cry

life is no different
we keep asking why

MOTHER

she said she'll be there for me
as the age old banyan tree
like shadows that cling to you
and stick no matter what you do
she said she'll never go
a step without me in tow
like the hand that holds you strong
even when all goes wrong
she said she's by my side
and behind her smile I can hide
as sun rays when storm clouds break
my sorrows and tears she'll take
she said and did all she could
and perhaps she forever would
a dark night took her in a sweep
to unknown lands far and deep
and then in a flicker she was gone
a blown out candle the wicker torn
like images on a train-window fly
memories are all I now live by

ODE TO CANCER

under the barren sky
and veiled night
whispers death

whispers into my ears
caresses my shaky limbs
tired muscles
battle torn sinews
and cold blood in shadowy veins

I can hear the distant bell
from faraway lands
the call of death

I smell raw flesh burning
tongues of fire
devouring new born lives

steely gaze of faceless eyes
taunt and torture my frail frame
ravishes my soul
hell awaits me on the other side or heaven
I don't know

and then
the soothing touch

of angel lips
fleeting glance of mercy
and I smile my way
unto rusty death
young and spent

OF FAIRIES AND LAMPS

caressing the velvet sky
her hair spoke to the stars
of dark alleys in the galaxy
and milky way that lost
direction in the maze
of desire

and how once she was
a child of the universe
before the lamp imprisoned
her in its sooty womb
only to be freed by the touch
of a magic hand
yet to be born

curse of a black night
she said and sins of a
thousand years

OF THOUGHTS AND UNSPOKEN WORDS

poised over the trigger
a thought hung like the
suicide bomber
calm and confused
to form into words
a whiplash
caged thunderbolts
release was a twitching tongue
away

the mind fought
nervous in the knowledge that
the all consuming fury
is a merciless fellow and
may leave you only half
dead to suffer alone in
an untold hell

the image shook the thought
faltering it shrank into the hidden
depths of sanity and silence
far away from its perpetrators and
victims alike
scared

not anymore sure of
who's right and what
is wrong

and relieved

the sun rose to see another day
in a bright blue sky

ON A WINTER NIGHT

the dark despair of the winter night
settled on his skin like an old
worn blanket and chilled the brittle bones to
unknown numbness

trembling in the eerie silence
his rickety breath struggled for freedom
and formed ghostly images in the air
in the corner the kettle whizzed out a
sorry goodbye and retired

a lone lizard stuck on the wall
watched him with ferocious intensity

he looked for warmth and touch of flesh
love
there was none left
time takes its toll
like a forest fire
ravaged
he waited for the other side
a cruel winter chill and frost on his lips
for company.

and a lizard with eyes that saw
everything and nothing

ORANGE MOON

when you see the orange moon
know that fever is not far away

delirium will take your confused mind
to the truth you always looked for

ALL THAT MATTERS

a day gone without a drop
of blood on the floor
or a blade changing shape of
a tree or a stone's contour
rivers ran wherever they can
and skies were back to blue
wars were lost at no one's cost and
all that mattered was you

POETRY OF DECADENCE

he sat with his awards
unrewarding pieces of metal
and memories of paltry sums
long spent
dwelling on stale cabbage
and the foul smelling stove
missus let out a sermon on
husbandry that poetry could not
digest but chewed on
the dank room devoid of muses
cried for solitude and miracles
he thought of the deadlines
publishers and landlord
unpaid bills
the cry of the new born
poorly fed
his pen would not crawl
sheets of white lying dead at feet
scribbled
cancelled and torn
like so many wars civilizations
fought and justified
epics
or epitome of dead minds

REFLECTIONS ON TIME

years go by and mosses
grow over
footprints and memories
and books by the cover
that we read sitting close
hands held taught
of angels and demons
and how they fought
little did we know
that it was really us
angels make fairy tales and
devil rules the dust
and a clock stopped somewhere
and a bell died in chime
and dust is where we all
find peace with time

RUST

do not let rust
settle on your shackles
music will die inside

polluted iron will be with you forever
devouring
like ants on a carcass

SHADOWS OF OBLIVION

returning to oblivion
he left his shadow behind
against the silhouette of a fading sun

the approaching night
swallowed it and all that
remained was a void

a lone owl perched in silence
sat wide-eyed and witnessed the disappearance
bemused

it watched its own nervous shadow
melt into the night

SILENCE

let the lines remain buried
forgotten

let words drown
in the cacophony
of ocean
deep and silenced

let syllables loose
their way in the
desert storm
never to be found again

let me listen to the
rustle of falling leaves
of voices dying in distance
of the approaching
slumber

let silence sing its
own love song

SPEAKING OF SILENCE

in a world full of emptiness
the only sound was of silence
and it spoke through silhouettes
of unspoken words
your lips lost in the rains
drowned in an unknown river

I learned to speak silence
ghosts of long dead words
voices forever have waylaid

STORY

I saw her
footprints

long after
she crossed
the road

TEAR DROP

inconspicuous as it was
a tiny speck
rolled over the brim
and cascaded down
a single tear

a symphony of pain
a silent scream
if you listen
in it you can hear

TEARS OF HEAVEN

walking by the dried fields
scorched by a cruel summer sun
she cried for the burnt
blades of grass
crucified in untold agony

and tear by tear she fed life
into them
each drop a gift from the clouds that gave
birth to the rivers

like a phoenix
reborn

THE BRIDGE

I forfeited my pain
to your happiness
to see the night sky
in your eyes
stars sparkling in
memory of love

your unspoken words
like the summer breeze
wafted away
lost forever

the bridge remained alone
forgotten
it never found footsteps
again

THE FIGHT

orange rage glowed like burning embers
fiery thoughts leapt and chased
the breeze and fireflies
you could almost hear memories
crackling in the white heat
bridges were burnt in the silence of the night

the morning knew nothing about
it and went on with its business
like every other day
consumed in the thought of a golden moon
and dreams

only the river wept and her waves
carried the story of an unnecessary war
to the ocean
to hide it in the corals of time

THE JOURNEY

when I left
wind sighed
the overcast sky
shed a tear
the forest covered me
and the sea whispered
come let me take you

and I returned to the womb
from where the journey had begun
memoirs of ashes and fragments
I left behind
for the storyteller and beyond

THE KISS

the brush
tentative
shy almost
caressed the canvas
albeit furtively
and drew a kiss across the blood-red lips

smell of fresh paint and lust hung in the air
heavy in its labored breathing

the canvas returned the favor
stroke by stroke
in the haze of an unfinished dream

a story was born
of love and labor

THE MEETING

flickering in the distance
phosphorus-lined waves broke the
monotony of the night momentarily
and kissing the shore went back
to the dark depths of the ocean

a chance meeting
destined to an abrupt end
or a doomed affair to begin with
only time will tell

so told the moon
to the sky

THE PARTING

and they parted ways
no words
no goodbye
just a momentary turn of heads
eyes locked in denial

shadows travelling backwards
for one last kiss

THE SOUP BOWL

the soup bowl smacked of happy memories
tiny fragments of green on the ceramic
glistening with remnants of a sticky broth
sweet smell of corn lingered in the air
a single strand of carrot missed by the spoon
lay smug on the plate underneath
warm still

beyond the polished glass
his face pressed tight against the shine
he tried to remember his last meal

age has dulled his memory or hunger
he could not tell

THE STORM

no warning
no predicament
it came
taking everything in its wake
it roared through the by-lanes
and highways
trees bending low
murmured in protest
a flicker of fear in the eagle's eyes
and men hurrying home

then came the rain
hope of course
like the oft trodden grass
began its climb to find light again
and faith

THE VERDICT

a forest resort
autumn night
kebabs on the grill
we had a fight
the moon was confused
stars died in shame
morning after
excuses lame
and so it went
a trip on court's order
I crossed the line
you crossed the border
wine it must be
wicked in desire
crackling logs aflame
the solemn fire
thirty-grand a night
it did cost
but we found the river
that we lost

TIME

can you measure how long someone will be sad
or happy
how long does it take for tears to dry
or for a smile to fade

if pain refuses to leave and clings on
it becomes your skin
will you call it timeless

or a clock that ran out of time

VOID

peels of fading dusk
scrappy in its light
entering through
the cracked window pane
probed the black boundaries
of his world
fragmented pieces of life
illuminated like a silver strand
amidst the assorted darkness
corner of a writer's desk
edge of the rocking chair
now in now out
closed door in the backdrop
and rickety fingers
poised over a pen that
never wrote

and then
twilight merged
with evening
and he retired into his darkness
not a line written
no story to tell

WHEELCHAIR

sitting in the balcony
north wind in her face
she looked at her everyday road
in her mind she knew
right after the bend
leaving behind the city
and its congested breath
the road meandered towards the mysterious
savanna and the land of the Masai
majestic and unconquered
mountains rising high
above the skyscrapers
dwarfed them almost
into insignificance making her smile
in her backyard the great Amazon spread
her fauna in absolute abundance
her feet touching moss on the forest floor
she strained her ears and the Mediterranean
called out her name
she could taste salt in the air
oh
how she wished to go under the blue waves
and come out a mermaid

but all that have to wait
she told herself

her practiced hands turning
the wheelchair in a smooth arc
and she went back to the four walls
her world for all these years and
keeper of her dreams

WORDSMITH

in ragged tee and jeans
his age-old sneakers screaming abuse
he tottered from door to door
looking for words
an alphabet here
some broken pieces there
seeds

he planted them in his thoughts
feeding them with care
nurturing them with love and
despair until they grew up to be the poem
he always wanted to be
written on his epitaph